MW01611714

WAITING FOR THE BUS

A tragicomedy in one act by
Benjamin Connor

www.youthplays.com
info@youthplays.com
424-703-5315

Waiting for the Bus © 2017 Benjamin Connor
All rights reserved. ISBN 978-1-62088-750-9.

Caution: This play is fully protected under the copyright laws of the United States of America, Canada, the British Commonwealth and all other countries of the copyright union and is subject to royalty for all performances including but not limited to professional, amateur, charity and classroom whether admission is charged or presented free of charge.

Reservation of Rights: This play is the property of the author and all rights for its use are strictly reserved and must be licensed by the author's representative, YouthPLAYS. This prohibition of unauthorized professional and amateur stage presentations extends also to motion pictures, recitation, lecturing, public reading, radio broadcasting, television, video and the rights of adaptation or translation into non-English languages.

Performance Licensing and Royalty Payments: Amateur and stock performance rights are administered exclusively by YouthPLAYS. No amateur, stock or educational theatre groups or individuals may perform this play without securing authorization and royalty arrangements in advance from YouthPLAYS. Required royalty fees for performing this play are available online at www.YouthPLAYS.com. Royalty fees are subject to change without notice. Required royalties must be paid each time this play is performed and may not be transferred to any other performance entity. All licensing requests and inquiries should be addressed to YouthPLAYS.

Author Credit: All groups or individuals receiving permission to produce this play must give the author(s) credit in any and all advertisements and publicity relating to the production of this play. The author's billing must appear directly below the title on a separate line with no other accompanying written matter. The name of the author(s) must be at least 50% as large as the title of the play. No person or entity may receive larger or more prominent credit than that which is given to the author(s) and the name of the author(s) may not be abbreviated or otherwise altered from the form in which it appears in this Play.

Publisher Attribution: All programs, advertisements, flyers or other printed material must include the following notice:
Produced by special arrangement with YouthPLAYS (www.youthplays.com).

Prohibition of Unauthorized Copying: Any unauthorized copying of this book or excerpts from this book, whether by photocopying, scanning, video recording or any other means, is strictly prohibited by law. This book may only be copied by licensed productions with the purchase of a photocopy license, or with explicit permission from YouthPLAYS.

Trade Marks, Public Figures & Musical Works: This play may contain references to brand names or public figures. All references are intended only as parody or other legal means of expression. This play may also contain suggestions for the performance of a musical work (either in part or in whole). YouthPLAYS has not obtained performing rights of these works unless explicitly noted. The direction of such works is only a playwright's suggestion, and the play producer should obtain such permissions on their own. The website for the U.S. copyright office is *http://www.copyright.gov*.

COPYRIGHT RULES TO REMEMBER

1. To produce this play, you must receive prior written permission from YouthPLAYS and pay the required royalty.

2. You must pay a royalty each time the play is performed in the presence of audience members outside of the cast and crew. Royalties are due whether or not admission is charged, whether or not the play is presented for profit, for charity or for educational purposes, or whether or not anyone associated with the production is being paid.

3. No changes, including cuts or additions, are permitted to the script without written prior permission from YouthPLAYS.

4. Do not copy this book or any part of it without written permission from YouthPLAYS.

5. Credit to the author and YouthPLAYS is required on all programs and other promotional items associated with this play's performance.

When you pay royalties, you are recognizing the hard work that went into creating the play and making a statement that a play is something of value. We think this is important, and we hope that everyone will do the right thing, thus allowing playwrights to generate income and continue to create wonderful new works for the stage.

Plays are owned by the playwrights who wrote them. Violating a playwright's copyright is a very serious matter and violates both United States and international copyright law. Infringement is punishable by actual damages and attorneys' fees, statutory damages of up to $150,000 per incident, and even possible criminal sanctions. **Infringement is theft. Don't do it.**

Have a question about copyright? Please contact us by email at info@youthplays.com or by phone at 424-703-5315. When in doubt, please ask.

CAST OF CHARACTERS

LEO, male, 15-18. An oddball high schooler with a passion for philosophy and a contemplative air about him. There are more layers to him than anyone has the time to peel away.

RYAN, male, 15-18. Leo's more grounded friend. He is helpful and honest, and madly in love with April.

APRIL, female, 15-18. A sweet, cheerful teenager who is happy to be alive. She has a rare kind of independence.

CASEY, female, 15-18. A quiet, introspective poetry nut who tends to be a spectator in the world of high school more often than a participant.

SCENE 1

(Morning. A lonely bus stop with several seats. Enter RYAN and LEO with backpacks.)

LEO: ...and so I think I'm a skeptic. I don't really know anything, do I? Descartes' argument about the unreliability of the senses really got to me. I don't have any proof, any real proof, that what I see around me actually exists. All I can say with any certainty is that *I* exist. Because if I don't exist, who's having the thought that I don't exist? Does that make sense?

RYAN: *(Snaps out of a daze:)* Yeah, definitely.

LEO: Were you listening to what I was saying?

RYAN: Yes.

LEO: OK, what was I saying?

(Beat.)

RYAN: No.

LEO: What is the point of talking if no one is going to listen?!

RYAN: Oh, I agree.

(They sit.)

LEO: You know the bus isn't gonna get here for another ten minutes. Can I at least finish my thought? It feels like I'm holding in a sneeze.

RYAN: If I say no—

LEO: OK, Descartes concluded that he knew, absolutely, that he existed...and that's all. But philosophers like G.E. Moore pointed out that Descartes was basically saying "no one can know the existence of anyone but themselves," and Moore said who was "no one" if not other people? So other people must...

(He notices that Ryan is staring into space.)

Ryan?

RYAN: Do you think they have gluten-free food at the carnival?

LEO: What?

RYAN: The carnival. This weekend. Do you think they have gluten-free food?

LEO: You know, I'm getting the weirdest feeling you still weren't listening.

RYAN: C'mon, this is serious. Do you think they have a stand, or like a food truck, with gluten-free food?

LEO: Why on Earth do you...you're not allergic to gluten!

RYAN: Well, no.

LEO: I didn't even know you were going to the carnival. Are you going with a friend who's allergic to gluten?

RYAN: Well, I mean, no. Not—

LEO: Oh my Lord, you have a date.

RYAN: No. No, that's not—I don't.

LEO: Oh, I could cry! Look at you! They grow up so fast.

RYAN: I don't have a date.

LEO: Well, then you want a date. I have a hard time believing that you're just expressing concern for the gluten-free carnival enthusiasts of the Tri-State Area. So who is it?

RYAN: Forget I asked.

LEO: Hmmm...nope, not gonna do that.

RYAN: Leo.

LEO: Oh, throw me a bone here! I get so little of the gossip, being—you know—a pariah.

RYAN: You're not a pariah.

LEO: You're sweet. Who's the gal?

RYAN: Please, Leo.

LEO: Or guy! Love is blind and all.

RYAN: It's a girl.

LEO: Oh, sure, he'll rise to *that* bait.

RYAN: This conversation is over.

LEO: Uh huh. I'm gonna find out who your mysterious celiac crush is, you know. I'm like Sherlock Holmes over here. Nothing gets by me.

RYAN: You are in no way like Sherlock Holmes.

LEO: I am too! I observe. I reflect. And then I deduce. Razor-sharp perception.

RYAN: Your fly's open.

LEO: Thank you. *(He zips it up.)* Fine, then, if you won't tell me...back to philosophy. I believe I was discussing Moore?

RYAN: And I was wishing you'd discuss less.

(Enter APRIL, with backpack. She is outgoing and happy to be alive.)

APRIL: Hi, boys. Who finished their history project?

RYAN: *(Groans.)* I'm like halfway done. I still have to make a PowerPoint about Julius Caesar and his accomplishments.

(April sits down.)

APRIL: What are his accomplishments?

(Beat.)

RYAN: Maybe less than halfway done.

APRIL: I don't know anything about my guy, yet, either. Haven't even started.

LEO: Would it put a damper on this little pity party if I said I'm finished?

RYAN: *Yes.*

APRIL: Ugh. Lucky.

LEO: I really can't see how luck has anything to do with it.

APRIL: You were born with a good work ethic. That's lucky.

LEO: John Locke would say that you aren't *born* with any qualities.

RYAN: And we're off...

LEO: He would say that you acquire all your personality traits after birth, as a result of your experiences.

RYAN: He would but he can't, because he's dead and irrelevant.

(April pulls out a bag of carrots and starts eating.)

Carrots?

APRIL: Mom woke me up late again. Didn't have time for breakfast. So...carrots.

LEO: *(Looks through his backpack:)* Oh, April, I think I have an oatmeal bar in here somewhere. You want that? Can't have you living like a rabbit here.

APRIL: Wish I could, but oatmeal has oats in it.

LEO: Well, yes.

APRIL: I'm gluten intolerant.

LEO: *(Slaps a hand to his cheek.)* Really? Well, I'll be. I never knew that.

APRIL: I kinda avoid mentioning it. But I thought you knew, actually. I mean, how long have we known each other? Middle school?

LEO: Elementary... *(He turns to Ryan:)* my dear Watson.

RYAN: *(Groans.)* Let's move on.

LEO: This is interesting! You learn new things every day! Right, Ryan?

RYAN: As long as you're alive you do.

APRIL: You boys alright?

LEO & RYAN: *(Leo cheerfully; Ryan bitterly:)* Yep!

(Enter CASEY, with backpack. She is quiet and contemplative.)

CASEY: Hi, everyone.

(Beat.)

APRIL: Oh — Casey! Hi! What are you — Why —

CASEY: My bus stop got moved. I live in this neighborhood, but my stop was all the way over on Calahan Street. So we got it moved here. So...hi. I'm here now.

APRIL: Well, welcome! Come sit right next to me.

(Casey sits.)

You know Ryan and Leo?

RYAN: Hi.

CASEY: Hi.

LEO: Hi.

CASEY: Hi.

(Long pause.)

APRIL: *(Quietly, to Casey:)* Yaaaayyyyy...

RYAN: So, April —

CASEY: Is that the bus?

APRIL: Yellow, has wheels. I vote yes.

(They start getting up.)

Casey, just so you know, our bus driver…

LEO: Is a war criminal in hiding.

RYAN: Nothing's been confirmed yet.

APRIL: The point is he's a little dictatorial with time.

LEO: Slightly pathological about arriving here and getting to school at the same time every day.

RYAN: The day he arrives late is the day the world ends.

(They all start walking out.)

APRIL: Hey, did you guys know that the carnival is this week?

(Exeunt omnes.)

SCENE 2

(The next morning, same bus stop. Enter Ryan and Leo.)

LEO: …and so Zeno defended this idea that motion was an illusion. He came up with a bunch of paradoxes that seemed to prove that movement is actually impossible.

RYAN: Is that why I can never get away from you?

LEO: Like there's one called Achilles and the Tortoise. Zeno says, let's assume that Achilles — great warrior and athlete that he is — can run one mile in the time it takes the tortoise to run one-tenth of a mile.

RYAN: I love how you skip the part where you ask if I care.

LEO: So Achilles runs this race against the tortoise, but because of the speed difference the tortoise gets a one-mile head start.

RYAN: Well, you know what they say about Achilles. He was always fair to the tortoises.

LEO: So Achilles runs one mile in the time it takes the tortoise to run one-tenth of a mile. Then, Achilles runs one-tenth of a mile in the time it takes the tortoise to run one-hundredth of a mile.

RYAN: Then, Achilles realizes he's competing with a reptile and rethinks his life choices.

LEO: The obvious result is that Achilles will never catch the tortoise, because whatever distance Achilles has to run to reach the tortoise, the tortoise will have run one-tenth of that distance further in that time.

RYAN: Alright, wait, stop. You're not making sense. Of course he'll catch it, I mean…he's faster! Right? Or is this where Achilles stops to sleep under a tree, and slow and steady wins the race?

(They sit.)

LEO: No, this is where unassailable logic doesn't match our observation in the real world. So the overall conclusion Zeno drew is that movement is an illusion.

(Ryan throws his hands in the air.)

RYAN: How are we having this—I get sucked in. I get sucked in every time, and by the end my life is a lie.

(Enter April.)

APRIL: Deep.

LEO: Hello, April.

APRIL: Hi, friends. How are we this morning?

RYAN: Fine. Although I still haven't finished the history project.

APRIL: Ah! I'm more worried about starting than finishing at this point.

RYAN: Leo, wasn't there something you had to do?

LEO: *(Stares.)* Nope.

RYAN: Leo, by any chance did you *forget something today?*

LEO: Oh! Yes! That's what it is. Yes, I've forgotten my lunch box! Whoops. I'd better go get that.

> *(He gets up to go.)*

What would I do without you, Ryan? *(To April:)* See how thoughtful he is? I'm gonna go.

> *(Exit Leo.)*

APRIL: That was bizarre.

RYAN: That was Leo. Hey—question for you.

APRIL: Shoot.

RYAN: Are you—I mean—are you busy on Saturday?

APRIL: *(Thinking:)* Saturday?

RYAN: It's totally fine if you are. More than fine. Very very fine.

APRIL: Saturday's open for me. Why?

RYAN: Uh, well, because I was going to go to the carnival that day.

> *(They stare at each other, both waiting for the other to speak.)*

APRIL: I…support that decision?

RYAN: Well, yeah, no, I was wondering if…

APRIL: If…?

RYAN: …if you also wanted to go.

APRIL: If I wanted to go…with you?

RYAN: Yes. Sorry. Poorly worded.

APRIL: Yes.

RYAN: "Yes," it was poorly worded, or—?

APRIL: Yes, I would love to go to the carnival—with you—on Saturday.

(Beat.)

RYAN: OK. Great! I mean, not great. Just…just cool. Good. Copacetic.

APRIL: It sounds fun! I hear they have a gluten-free food truck.

RYAN: Yeah. OK then. Saturday.

APRIL: *(Smiles:)* Saturday.

(There is an awkward silence for several seconds. Enter Leo and Casey. Casey has a book.)

LEO: …and so Zeno's conclusion was that—

CASEY: That movement was impossible.

LEO: Well, yeah, actually. See, Ryan, here's someone who cares.

RYAN: Don't let him bore you too much, Casey. I think there's an off button on the back of his neck.

(April laughs.)

There's the bus.

(They stand.)

APRIL: God, the punctuality is scary.

(April and Casey exit, Ryan is still gathering his stuff and Leo waits for him.)

LEO: So?!

RYAN: Let's just say the phrase "gluten-free food truck" was said.

LEO: Hey!!

(The boys high five, then exit.)

SCENE 3

(Monday morning of the next week. Guess where? Bus stop. Enter Ryan and Leo.)

LEO: You have to tell me.

RYAN: I really don't.

LEO: You *have* to tell me. You can't just dangle words like that and then shut down.

RYAN: Words like what?

LEO: Like *"disaster."*

RYAN: Oh, come on.

LEO: You called it a "disaster"!

RYAN: It was.

LEO: Yeah, OK, but now I've got this mental picture of a hurricane, a tornado sweeping through the carnival. April getting eaten by a shark or something.

RYAN: Don't joke about it.

LEO: Don't joke about April getting eaten by a shark? I feel like that's fair game, honestly…

RYAN: Will you shut up?

LEO: Listen, dates go badly sometimes. I would imagine. You'll feel better when you talk about it out loud.

(The boys sit.)

RYAN: You need to promise not to talk to anyone about this.

LEO: *Please.* I don't talk to anyone, period.

RYAN: I'm serious.

LEO: And I'm a pariah. C'mon, we're losing daylight.

RYAN: *(Sighs:)* Alright. Listen — it's just — it's not exactly one of those things that makes me sound good. As a person. The whole thing makes me seem —

LEO: *Tell the story.*

RYAN: It's bad.

LEO: It can't be that bad.

RYAN: We got into a car accident.

(Leo is stunned into silence.)

Yeah. Thanks.

LEO: Well — wait. It doesn't have to be that bad. A little tap... You hit your mirror on a sign in the parking lot...

RYAN: I hit a truck.

LEO: You hit a *truck*? Oh, God. Is April OK? Are you OK? Well, you seem fine, or else you wouldn't be here. Is April OK? Heck, is the truck driver OK? What about the insurance company, are they OK?

RYAN: Will you calm down?!

LEO: Is April OK?

RYAN: I thought she was fine at first. We just kinda hit it and both of us shot forward. And we pulled over and got out of the car and we were OK and fine and everything, but then she just started crying.

LEO: Oh, no.

RYAN: And I think her hand really hurt. Sprained or something. It was—it was probably the airbag. I don't know. But I really thought it was all gonna be fine—the truck guy was actually a truck lady and she was really nice, and the car doesn't look that bad, it kinda looks like Picasso's version of a Honda Civic—but April.

LEO: Is she OK?

RYAN: Her mom came and picked her up, and they said they were gonna go to a clinic to check out her hand. It was all very, very tranquil. Like everyone thought I was gonna lose it, so they were all acting really calm just for me.

LEO: Was this on the way to—

RYAN: No, coming back. After an amazing day.

LEO: Right.

RYAN: She texted me that nothing was broken. On Saturday. We haven't talked since.

LEO: OK. *(Beat.)* I don't think your date went very well.

RYAN: Oh God, Leo, she's gonna be here any minute.

LEO: It wasn't your fault, was it? The—you know…

RYAN: Accident, Leo. The accident. I'm not a trauma victim. And no, I don't think so. But I'm a minor; I was behind the other car. I'm gonna get blamed for it anyway.

LEO: Yeah, maybe.

RYAN: This is gonna be a really awkward morning.

LEO: No, it won't! Not at all!

(Ryan looks at him.)

Maybe a little.

RYAN: Auugghhh.

LEO: Wanna change the subject?

RYAN: Yes, please.

LEO: OK, so —

RYAN: Leo?

LEO: Yeah?

RYAN: If philosophy is mentioned, a vein will pop out of my neck sideways.

LEO: Noted. So…the history project?

RYAN: Aaaah, yeah. I finished my PowerPoint last night while I was wallowing in my sorrow.

LEO: Who's your person again?

RYAN: Julius Caesar.

LEO: You're kidding. Really?

RYAN: No, why?

LEO: You've got the best one.

RYAN: What do you mean, "the best one"?

(Enter Casey, carrying a poster board.)

CASEY: Who's the best one?

RYAN: Hi, Casey.

LEO: Julius Caesar is.

RYAN: Really? 'Cause my lengthy midnight research shows that he was a dusty old consul who did a lot less than everyone thinks he did.

LEO: No, you don't get it! It's about the legacy. Everyone knows who Julius Caesar is. Everyone. In the world. You'd have to live under a rock not to. But he died *2000 years ago.* Isn't that incredible? He walked the Earth 2000 years ago and we're still talking about him.

RYAN: Some of us are, anyway.

LEO: My point is, plenty of people are famous enough to be known by everyone. Jesus, Napoleon, Hitler. But none of them have been around as long as Caesar. He is the oldest famous person. Longest shelf life. That's why he's the best.

RYAN: Huh. That's—I guess it's impressive.

LEO: I want to be the next Julius Caesar. I mean, not the murder and war and getting-stabbed-by-all-of-your-friends stuff. But the fame. I want to do something so people are still talking about me in 2000 years.

CASEY: Still quoting you.

RYAN: Yeah, "Veni, vidi, vici."

LEO: "Et tu, Brute?"

CASEY: Words named after you…kaiser, czar…

RYAN: The month of July. The Julian calendar.

LEO: Caesarean sections.

CASEY: Plays written about you.

LEO: Cults devoted to you.

CASEY: And we're talking about him right now.

   (Beat.)

RYAN: Holy crap, I've got the best one.

LEO: And Leo was vindicated forevermore.

CASEY: Is April not coming today?

RYAN: I don't know.

LEO: I don't think she is.

CASEY: Oh.

LEO: I like the poster board. Vintage.

CASEY: *(Laughs:)* Thanks. Our computer broke a few months ago, so…poster board's been my friend.

(She shows Leo the poster board.)

My project's on Abigail Adams.

RYAN: I should text her.

LEO: *(To Ryan:)* Abigail Adams?

(Ryan looks at him.)

Oh. Right. *(To Casey:)* Sounds interesting.

RYAN: Maybe I shouldn't.

LEO: Maybe you just should calm down.

CASEY: The bus is here.

RYAN: Oh, hell.

(They stand.)

LEO: Let's go.

(They grab their bags and exit.)

SCENE 4

(Two mornings later. Everyone's favorite bus stop. Enter Ryan, alone. He is on the phone.)

RYAN: No. Emily, I'm really fine. *(Beat.)* I'm fine! Really! A couple hundred. Yeah, exactly! I got lucky! *(Beat.)* Well, no, not lucky. *(Beat.)* Mom's worried about me, that's how she is. *(Beat.)* I guess she thought a casual call from a sibling would cheer me up. *(Beat.)* Yeah. You remember her, right? *(Beat.)* Well, she hurt her hand. *(Beat.)* I think she's gonna be OK. *(Beat.)* I know. I haven't even thought about that part yet. It's just—awkward. Anyway, thanks for calling, Em. *(Beat.)* It's not a big deal. I appreciate it. *(Beat.)* Don't you have college-y things to do? Lecture halls and sorority hazing? *(Beat.)* Great. *(Beat.)* Goodbye, Em.

(He goes and sits down. Enter Leo.)

LEO: It is *cold* today. I thought we were done with that.

RYAN: Yep.

LEO: *(Sits.)* So. How are you?

RYAN: *(Musing:)* She'll be here in a few minutes. And every morning for the rest of the year.

LEO: Yep. And next year.

RYAN: And then we go off to college.

LEO: And then you'll meet new people.

RYAN: I think I've destroyed any chance of ever getting off the ground with April.

LEO: Oh, come on.

RYAN: I think I've ruined a friendship, too.

LEO: Yeah, but it wasn't really a friendship, was it? I mean, you weren't going to be content with friendship. You weren't happy.

RYAN: I was happy. I was definitely *happier.*

LEO: I don't see how you can want something you don't have like that *and* be happy.

RYAN: *(Looks at him.)* Have you ever *really* fallen for a girl, Leo?

LEO: *(Laughs.)* I'm a robot, silly. No human emotion.

RYAN: See, but you're not…

LEO: We don't want to talk about this.

RYAN: *You* don't want to talk about this?

LEO: No, *we* don't want to talk about this.

RYAN: Leo, are you telling me there is a girl?

LEO: This is always a fun game to play.

RYAN: You know, if you tell me —

LEO: Then everything will magically fall into place?

RYAN: I would never tell a soul.

LEO: Neither would I. I'm not the focus around here, Ryan. I'm the supporting character. I don't count.

RYAN: You count!

LEO: Listen, I'm not — I'm not that type of teenager. I'm not that type of person.

RYAN: What type of person?

LEO: The type that lets their secrets spill. The type that opens up. *(Beat.)* No one knows who I am, you know.

RYAN: That's not true! Everybody knows you!

LEO: Everyone knows a little bit of me. No one really gets close.

RYAN: What about me? I'm your friend.

LEO: Do I have any pets?

RYAN: What?

LEO: Do I have any pets? What'd I do this summer? What'd I get for my birthday? When *is* my birthday? Favorite TV show, favorite book, dream job? *(Beat.)* We're bus stop acquaintances. And it isn't your fault. It's mine, remember? I spend more time trying to figure myself out than I do giving anyone else a chance.

RYAN: You changed the subject. We were talking about your mystery romance.

LEO: I'm a smart kid, Ryan. Trust me when I say we don't want to talk about this.

(They sit in silence.)

Nothing to be done...

(Ryan stands up.)

RYAN: You know, you baffle me. You really do. You complain about how no one knows you, and then you refuse to tell. Here I am! I'm your friend! I wanna know more about you, and you don't open up!

LEO: I know.

RYAN: We sit here every morning, and we talk, and I don't know about *you*. We never talk about *you*.

LEO: I know.

RYAN: Well, now we're gonna talk about you. Favorite book, favorite movie, favorite Disney princess, whatever. *And,* first, if you could date any girl you know, hypothetically, who would she be? Your dream gal. Go.

LEO: *(Wryly:)* Her name's April. Maybe you know her.

(Long silence.)

RYAN: Oh, crap.

LEO: Well, that about sums it up, doesn't it?

RYAN: I don't really know what to say.

LEO: I think at this point protocol dictates that you challenge me to a duel.

RYAN: Jesus, Leo. You never said anything.

LEO: What would I have said?

RYAN: I was talking your ear off about—about her, and—Jesus, Leo.

LEO: It's fine. I was happy to listen. I learned a couple things.

RYAN: You don't really feel like no one knows you, do you?

LEO: I feel like...I give every person I meet a slightly different version of Leo. No one's collected them all.

RYAN: That's fair. But there's nothing wrong with that.

LEO: *(Laughs.)* There's nothing wrong with being lonely as long as you have more time, sure. But I'm worried about dying. I'm worried about after I die, when everyone at the funeral says how great I was and then they all struggle to remember exactly what I was like. I'm worried about the obituary where they fail to mention my passions 'cause they couldn't remember any. I'm worried because I haven't entrusted anyone else with a complete blueprint of who I am. Forget 2000 years. If I got hit by a bus today, Ryan, I wouldn't last twenty.

RYAN: You know that isn't true. You *know* that isn't true. God, Leo, you think too much. You're unhappy because you're overthinking life.

LEO: Overthinking life. There's a feat.

RYAN: I hope it felt good to get...whatever that was off your chest.

LEO: Yep.

    (Beat.)

RYAN: This is gonna be a really awkward morning.

LEO: *(Smiles.)* Nothing to be done about that, either.

RYAN: Oh, hell.

LEO: *(Snapping out of it:)* Relax. I'm fine. You and April will be fine. You're both embarrassed. You're both —

   (Enter April, with a cast on her hand.)

APRIL: God, I almost missed it again.

RYAN: Nope. We're just sitting here and waiting.

APRIL: *(Sits.)* Great.

RYAN: Are you — How's your hand?

APRIL: It's gonna be fine. You don't have to look so worried.

RYAN: I feel horrible.

APRIL: Don't. I wanted to —

   (Enter Casey.)

Hi, Casey!

CASEY: Hi. You have a cast!

APRIL: That I do; nothing to worry about. How are you?

CASEY: Me? Freezing.

LEO: You kidding? It's a sauna compared to yesterday.

CASEY: I'm always cold.

RYAN: *(To April:)* What were you saying?

LEO: You don't have a jacket.

CASEY: Oh. No. Yeah. I know I have one somewhere, but it isn't — well, it isn't here.

APRIL: *(To Ryan:)* Maybe later?

LEO: For God's sake, you're shivering.

(Leo reaches into his backpack and pulls out a jacket. Hands it to Casey wordlessly.)

CASEY: Oh. Thanks.

(She slips on the jacket and takes out her book.)

LEO: I see we've moved on to poetry.

APRIL: I love a good poem! Read us something.

CASEY: Oh, you don't want to hear this stuff. It's all grim.

RYAN: Sounds perfect.

CASEY: OK…here, you read it.

(She gives the book to Leo.)

LEO: *(Flipping through the pages.)* Whenever Richard Cory went down town
We people on the pavement looked at him:
He was a gentleman from sole to crown,
Clean favored, and imperially slim.

And he was rich — yes, richer than a king —
And admirably schooled in every grace:
In fine, we thought that he was everything
To make us wish that we were in his place.

So on we worked, and waited for the light,
And went without the meat, and cursed the bread;
And Richard Cory, one calm summer night,
Went home and put a bullet through his head.

RYAN: Cheery.

CASEY: I said it was grim. That's the bus.

(They stand.)

RYAN: Coulda seen that one coming.

(April laughs.)

LEO: Same as always.

(They exit. Casey is the last one to leave.)

SCENE 5

(The next morning. Deepest, darkest Africa. Or a bus stop. Director's choice. Enter Ryan and Leo.)

LEO: ...it's something called the "subjective character of experience." Nagel was basically saying that you can never truly know what it's like to be someone else. You can't step into anyone else's self, you can only imagine yourself in their place.

RYAN: Are there any philosophers who expressed themselves entirely in silence?

LEO: You know, I thought you might be more interested in Nagel than the others.

RYAN: *(Sits.)* You kidding? Nagel's my favorite.

LEO: *(Sits.)* Yeah, OK. I thought you might be more interested because...I think you're feeling very alone right now. It might help you to understand that no one can ever understand you—

RYAN: Upbeat.

LEO: —but that no one understands anyone, so it's fine.

RYAN: Leo, I think we're gonna cross "marriage counselor" off the career list.

LEO: You do it, too, you know.

RYAN: I do what?

LEO: You don't let anyone in. You make all these witty little remarks, but you don't talk about anything serious. You're hiding, too.

RYAN: OK. Fine. Tell me more about Nagel.

LEO: He says that no one could ever duplicate your experiences, and between species you couldn't even come close. For example, if you wanted to know what it's like to be a bat —

RYAN: What?

LEO: What?

RYAN: Why would you ever want to know what it's like to be a bat?

LEO: It's an examp —

RYAN: Who's this weird Nagel guy, going around saying "Gee, what if we were bats? They're so cool."

LEO: He was just —

RYAN: Nagel probably got kicked out of philosophy club 'cause everyone else wanted to talk about the meaning of life and he was all "Excuse me, I'd like to discuss the bats."

LEO: *Ryan.*

RYAN: Sorry.

LEO: Anyway —

RYAN: I mean, if you're gonna wonder about any animal's consciousness, make it a cool one. Like a jaguar. Or a lemur.

LEO: Oh my god.

RYAN: Philosophy would be a lot more interesting if it were centered around lemurs.

LEO: *Seriously*—OK, never mind. Forget it. Didn't we just have a conversation about defense mechanisms?

RYAN: I've got nothing to defend.

LEO: 'Zat so? I think you're a little sadder than you're letting on.

RYAN: Why are we talking about me? Didn't we say we were gonna talk about you?

LEO: As usual: nothing to talk about.

RYAN: We sorta got sidetracked yesterday. I still wanted to ask you…where you stand on April.

LEO: I stand where I've stood for years. Far, far away.

RYAN: So you're not gonna—

LEO: I have no plans to stand any closer, if that's what you're asking.

RYAN: OK.

   (There is a long silence.)

LEO: Nothing to be done.

RYAN: You keep saying that like you don't have any hope left! Stop it! There's plenty to be hopeful about. You've got an admirer, y'know…

LEO: What?

RYAN: You're the Sherlock Holmes around here, right? I'm sure you've noticed a certain literary critic leaning in your direction.

LEO: Sorry?

RYAN: Come on! Am I not spelling this out? A touch of the poet? *(He motions toward Casey's seat.)* You really didn't pick up on that?

LEO: There's nothing to pick up on. Casey doesn't—I barely talk to her.

RYAN: She talks to you more than me or April.

LEO: You're crazy.

RYAN: I'm just saying, don't be surprised if you start getting anonymous sonnets in your locker…

LEO: First of all, she doesn't write poetry. She just likes to read it. She says when she puts pen to paper she always ends up writing something that's already been written.

RYAN: Did she confide this in you before or after you lent her your jacket like such a gentleman yesterday?

LEO: This conversation is over.

RYAN: Maybe you can be her poetic muse.

LEO: Maybe you can jump down a manhole.

RYAN: "Shall I compare thee to a summer's day, Leo?" …What rhymes with Leo? "Romeo," sort of, but the emphasis is wrong.

LEO: God Almighty.

(Enter April.)

APRIL: Is he bothering you, Leo?

LEO: All day, every day.

RYAN: Just giving Leo a sample of the poetry he can expect to receive in the coming weeks.

APRIL: You noticed it, too! I think that's fantastic, Leo. You're quite a catch.

LEO: Thanks.

RYAN: *(Realizing what Leo is thinking:)* It's not—I mean, there's no pressure.

LEO: Yeah. *(He stands, and picks up his backpack.)* You two are gonna want a couple minutes alone. This is where supporting characters take a walk.

(Exit Leo.)

APRIL: Oh...thanks. *(She sits.)* What's with him?

RYAN: I think...subjective character of experience.

APRIL: What?

RYAN: Nothing. He's just...feeling some empathy for Casey.

APRIL: I feel bad for him sometimes. It doesn't seem like he has many friends.

RYAN: He has me... He has you.

APRIL: Sure, but you know what I mean. Not that kind of "friends."

RYAN: We're not the right kind of friends?

APRIL: Well, come on! Has it ever felt like we were on the same...level as him? He's...a different crowd. God, I don't know how to describe it.

RYAN: *(Annoyed:)* Maybe you should stop trying.

APRIL: *(Taken aback:)* What's wrong?

RYAN: I don't know; it's just frustrating, the way you—I don't know.

APRIL: I'm not trying to be mean—

RYAN: But it's the way you think about him. It's like Achilles and the tortoise. We got the head start and he's never gonna... The way we think about him, we won't let him catch up.

APRIL: I don't know what you're saying.

RYAN: Forget it. Just forget the whole thing.

(They sit in silence for a moment.)

You don't know his favorite book. Favorite movie, anything. He could be our friend, on the same level as us, whatever the hell that is, if some of us didn't write him off.

APRIL: Are you mad at me? *(Realizing:)* You're mad at me! I didn't—what did I do? I just said it's hard to think of him as…close to us, because he's so different. I'm sure he thinks about us the same way.

RYAN: You know, the funny thing is I'm absolutely certain he doesn't.

APRIL: I'm sorry. I don't want to fight with you. We've got…other things to talk about.

RYAN: Oh, you wanna talk about us. Well, maybe you and me aren't the people we need to be talking about. Maybe I'm more worried about Leo.

APRIL: More worried about Leo? How many car accidents do I need to get into?

(They stare at each other. Enter Casey.)

CASEY: I'm sorry—I'm interrupting.

APRIL: No, it's fine, Casey. C'mon, sit down.

(Casey sits.)

RYAN: Yeah, join us, Casey! Got any more poems, like yesterday's? What was it called?

CASEY: *(Warily:)* "Richard Cory."

RYAN: "Richard Cory"! God, what a weird one. A guy who's hurting inside…and a world where nobody cares? *(Laughs.)* No, I think if Richard were here today—

APRIL: Is this some kind of veiled attack?

RYAN: Oh, I'm sorry. Am I veiling it?

CASEY: I'm definitely interrupting.

RYAN: You're not.

   (April stares at the ground.)

CASEY: *(Changing the subject:)* Where's Leo?

RYAN: He went for a walk. He'll be back.

CASEY: Don't want him to miss it.

APRIL: He knows when the bus'll be here; we don't have to worry about him.

RYAN: *(Laughs.)* No, we never really have to worry about him if we don't want to.

   (April looks up.)

APRIL: *What is this?!* What did I do? I didn't hurt him!

   (Ryan is silent.)

Know what? Forget it. There's the bus.

   (April stands. Casey turns to look.)

CASEY: It's here?

RYAN: April—

   (April grabs her stuff.)

APRIL: No. Not now.

   (Exit April. Casey and Ryan stand.)

CASEY: He isn't coming, is he?

RYAN: No…no, I don't think he is. He might've gone home.

CASEY: I—wanted to talk to him. You think he'll be here tomorrow?

   (Ryan looks at the place where Leo left.)

RYAN: You know, I have no idea.

(They exit.)

(End of play.)

The Author Speaks

What inspired you to write this play?
Waiting for the Bus is more autobiographical than I'd like to admit. It's always been beaten over my head that "write what you know" is the path to sincere work, so I took it to heart when I began *Waiting*. I'm a nut for philosophy and history, so both of those disciplines are woven through the play. And I know that some of the plaintive loneliness my characters express came from an emotional journey I had actually taken. *Waiting* is a dramatic manifestation of me, and that need for self-expression is what drove me to write it.

Was the structure or other elements of the play influenced by any other work?
I tend to start my creative work with a title, so the phrase *Waiting for the Bus* sprang to mind before I even began to write. This seemed too reminiscent of *Waiting for Godot* to ignore, and neither Samuel Beckett nor I were planning on changing our titles, so I waited until seeing a production of *Godot* before moving forward. I hoped to add some meaning to the fact that the titles were so similar. My play is not overly influenced by Beckett, but seeing *Godot* did inspire me to translate some of Didi and Gogo's hopeless, cyclical stagnancy to a group of people I could better relate to: teenagers.

Have you dealt with the same theme in other works that you have written?
My play *Direct Intervention* deals in part with the same obsession over legacy that appears in *Waiting for the Bus*. In fact, Julius Caesar is also mentioned in that work as history's oldest famous person. In addition, I wrote a short story called "The Jungle" in which the concept of how the protagonist will be remembered drives his actions. I don't know quite why this theme keeps coming back when I write; I think I might share

some of the fear of being forgotten that's imbued in my characters.

What writers have had the most profound effect on your style?
Aaron Sorkin and Stephen Sondheim are my top two. Both are sharp, purposeful writers who almost can't prevent themselves from pouring out the creativity they have to offer. Sondheim especially has a definite thematic goal in mind when he writes, and his musicals seem designed to make a larger point clear through the flaws and musings of his characters. Sorkin has taught me that my job is never to cater to the lowest common denominator; it's my job to raise it.

What do you hope to achieve with this work?
Broadly, the goal of my playwriting is to make somebody *feel* something. If I've elicited whatever emotion was intended from the audience, I feel I've done my job. But specifically in reference to *Waiting for the Bus*, I'd like someone in the audience to recognize themselves in one of the characters. The characters in *Waiting* are archetypes for more general personalities, so I think it's fairly easy to classify oneself as akin to one of the four teenagers in the show. From there, I hope that this play will make audience think more deeply about the way we treat each other.

What were the biggest challenges involved in the writing of this play?
I threw a million ideas into the pot for this play, and the biggest challenge was to synthesize these ideas into some kind of unified concept. Every play needs a theme, and *Waiting* had about fifteen of them in the first draft. I think I've whittled it down to six or seven since then.

What are the most common mistakes that occur in productions of your work?

I really can't criticize the actors that I've seen perform my work. My dialogue does tend to be wordy, so I'd advise actors to get their characters into a place where they can feel natural delivering some long and complicated lines.

What inspired you to become a playwright?

At first, playwriting was a convenient way to have my writing heard and legitimized. The first time I heard my words onstage, though, I was hooked on the feeling. Since then I've been chasing the prospect of having an effect on a whole crowd of people, of being able to float ideas to large groups as a way of making my voice heard. We all want to be noticed; this is how I do it.

How did you research the subject?

I went to school! Being around teenagers every day made it very easy to write four of them into a play. The four kids in *Waiting* don't share the interests of the typical teenager, though, and that's where additional research came in. I've taken a course in philosophy, so inserting the basic tenets of Zeno, Locke, and Descartes just required a quick brushing up on the finer points of their arguments. It took some informal polling to land on Julius Caesar as history's oldest famous person, since I had to make sure the Average Joe didn't consider Genghis Khan to be more important.

Are any characters modeled after real life or historical figures?

All four characters are modeled after me in some way or another, but Leo is the most distilled version of me that I've ever written. Ryan and April share some generalized traits with two of my friends, and the Ryan-April-Leo triangle is drawn from real life.

What is your writing process?

The process varies depending on the play, but with *Waiting for the Bus* I began with a plot outline. I knew how I wanted each scene to progress, and from there it was just a matter of turning these outlines into dialogue.

Shakespeare gave advice to the players in *Hamlet*; if you could give advice to your cast what would it be?

Find your character. That's all this play is: characters. Figure out how he/she is different from real-life you. Each of the four people in *Waiting* have a distinct physicality, a different way of speaking, a different objective, and a different perspective on the things all four of them see. These characters can't be painted with a broad brush; they've got to be sketched in with minute detail.

About the Author

Benjamin Connor is a playwright from Wilmington, Delaware. His plays include *Ledgeside, Waiting for the Bus,* and *Direct Intervention.* Ben's work has been produced and developed by the Town and Country Players, and his writing awards include prizes from the Princeton University 10-Minute Play Contest and the YouthPLAYS New Voices One-Act Competition. Ben is the recipient of a Scholastic National Gold Medal for his short story "The Oracle," which was published in Scholastic's annual *Best Teen Writing* periodical. Ben is also an actor and director, having performed with the Arden Shakespeare Guild, the Colonial Playhouse, Delaware All-State Theatre, and the Delaware Shakespeare Festival. In addition, Ben constructs crossword puzzles for the *Chronicle of Higher Education.*

About YouthPLAYS

YouthPLAYS (www.youthplays.com) is a publisher of award-winning professional dramatists and talented new discoveries, each with an original theatrical voice, and all dedicated to expanding the vocabulary of theatre for young actors and audiences. On our website you'll find one-act and full-length plays and musicals for teen and pre-teen (and even college) actors, as well as duets and monologues for competition. Many of our authors' works have been widely produced at high schools and middle schools, youth theatres and other TYA companies, both amateur and professional, as well as at elementary schools, camps, churches and other institutions serving young audiences and/or actors worldwide. Most are intended for performance by young people, while some are intended for adult actors performing for young audiences.

YouthPLAYS was co-founded by professional playwrights Jonathan Dorf and Ed Shockley. It began merely as an additional outlet to market their own works, which included a substantial body of award-winning published and unpublished plays and musicals. Those interested in their published plays were directed to the respective publishers' websites, and unpublished plays were made available in electronic form. But when they saw the desperate need for material for young actors and audiences—coupled with their experience that numerous quality plays for young people weren't finding a home—they made the decision to represent the work of other playwrights as well. Dozens and dozens of authors are now members of the YouthPLAYS family, with scripts available both electronically and in traditional acting editions. We continue to grow as we look for exciting and challenging plays and musicals for young actors and audiences.

About ProduceaPlay.com

Let's put up a play! Great idea! But producing a play takes time, energy and knowledge. While finding the necessary time and energy is up to you, ProduceaPlay.com is a website designed to assist you with that third element: knowledge.

Created by YouthPLAYS' co-founders, Jonathan Dorf and Ed Shockley, ProduceaPlay.com serves as a resource for producers at all levels as it addresses the many facets of production. As Dorf and Shockley speak from their years of experience (as playwrights, producers, directors and more), they are joined by a group of award-winning theatre professionals and experienced teachers from the world of academic theatre, all making their expertise available for free in the hope of helping this and future generations of producers, whether it's at the school or university level, or in community or professional theatres.

The site is organized into a series of major topics, each of which has its own page that delves into the subject in detail, offering suggestions and links for further information. For example, Publicity covers everything from Publicizing Auditions to How to Use Social Media to Posters to whether it's worth hiring a publicist. Casting details Where to Find the Actors, How to Evaluate a Resume, Callbacks and even Dealing with Problem Actors. You'll find guidance on your Production Timeline, The Theater Space, Picking a Play, Budget, Contracts, Rehearsing the Play, The Program, House Management, Backstage, and many other important subjects.

The site is constantly under construction, so visit often for the latest insights on play producing, and let it help make your play production dreams a reality.

More from YouthPLAYS

Me, My Selfie & I by Jonathan Dorf

Dramedy. 40-50 minutes (flexible). 2-20 females, 2-20+ males (6-40+ performers possible).

We live in a world of social media, one in which we seem to be recording our every experience. But are we making memories or missing out on them? Through a series of scenes and monologues—everything from an accidental first date to a most unusual art exhibit to creating that last, best selfie—we meet a group of teens who are struggling to find the balance between documenting their lives and living them.

Supermarket of Lost by Cassandra Hsiao

Drama. 15-20 minutes. 2 females, 1 male, 1 optional gender-flexible role.

Three young strangers collide at the Supermarket of Lost, a cosmic warehouse filled with the lost items of the world. As they explore the aisles and walk among people's memories, Austin, who is struggling with his past, connects with Hailee, who is struggling with her present. Accompanied by the young and spirited Violet, the two teens discover the difference between losing something and letting it go. Winner of the New Voices One-Act Competition for Young Playwrights.

The Superhero Ultraferno by Don Zolidis

Comedy. 100-110 minutes. 6-50 females, 6-50 males (12-90+ performers).

Now that nerds have taken over the world, it's imperative that all popular kids learn everything they can about comic book superheroes. Join two nerds and a crack team of actors as they race hilariously through the world of tights-wearing crimefighters, from the 1960s TV Batman to the soap opera insanity of the Fantastic Four to a bizarre, German opera of Spiderman. Also available as a one-act.

The Last Starfighter by Fred Landau (book) & Skip Kennon (music & lyrics)
Musical. 85-95 minutes. 6-30+ females, 9-30+ males (15-60+ performers possible).

Teenager Alex Rogan lives a hard-working, unrewarded life. But when he breaks the record for the video game in his trailer park, he discovers worlds he never knew existed—literally—and they are at war. With the Ko-Dan Armada threatening to overrun the forces of good, the video game's inventor, alien huckster Centauri, enlists Alex to fight for the Star League, leaving Beta, a body double droid, in his place. As the Beta does his often comically inept best to be a good "Alex"—all the while thwarting shape-shifting assassins—Alex soars through space as the universe's last hope. He'll need to reach deep within himself to discover his true potential and save us all. Also available in a 60-65 minute family-friendly version.

Rising by Arthur M. Jolly
Drama. 30-35 minutes. 4 females, 3 males.

Seven students are trapped in their Houston middle school classroom by rising floodwaters during Hurricane Harvey. As the waters rise, will they fall apart...or come together?

Medusa's Tale by Carol S. Lashof
Drama. 25-35 minutes. 3-4 females, 2 males (5-6 performers possible).

Countless would-be heroes have tried to slay Medusa, the famous monster with snakes for hair, but each and every one has turned to stone, simply by meeting her gaze. The young Perseus is different, though. The Goddess Athena has given him a sword and shield and told him to beware of Medusa's tricks. But Perseus finds himself suddenly unprepared when Medusa's weapon of choice is the story of her life. Will Perseus stay true to his course and slay the monster, or will the humanity of Medusa's tale slay the hero?

Whirligig by John Newman
Drama. 65-75 minutes. 2-21 females, 3-21 males (5-30+ performers possible).

After Brent Bishop gets drunk at a party, causes a car accident, and kills a young woman, the aftermath of his actions overwhelms him. Desperate to find a way to undo the suffering he's caused, Brent accepts the challenge from the victim's mother: build four whirligigs in the corners of the country as memorials to her daughter. As he takes his journey, four individuals he never meets find their lives transformed by the whirligigs he builds. But will the teen be able to forgive himself for an unforgivable mistake and move forward with his life?

Know Your Role by Brandi Owensby
Dramedy. 40-50 minutes (flexible). 5-25 females, 5-25 males (5-50 performers possible).

No sooner do we leave the womb than we're bombarded by society's expectations about gender. If you're a boy, you're like this. If you're a girl, you're like that. Whether it's how they dress, the rules of dating, body image, parental pressures or a host of other ways, through scenes and monologues that range from hilarious to heartbreaking, these teens reveal how gender expectations affect them and how they "role."

The Tea Servant by Ed Shockley
Drama. 30-35 minutes. 3+ males, 2+ females (5-25 performers possible).

Adapted from an anonymous Samurai legend, *The Tea Servant* is the tale of a serving girl whose impetuous princess is determined to travel alone to her lover. The servant dresses as a samurai to discourage robbers, but she is no fighter. When confronted on the road by a highwayman, the servant asks for time to deliver her mistress safe to the village and promises to return to duel. And when she does, her courage in facing death gains her far more than she could have imagined.

Made in the USA
Lexington, KY
13 November 2019

56937214R00024